Aaron
the Different

Aaron the Different

A story of courage, belonging, and acceptance

ETTY BURK

Academy Press

Copyright © 2022 Esther P. Burk. All rights reserved.

No part of this publication shall be reproduced, transmitted, or sold in whole or in part in any form without prior written consent of the author, except as provided by the United States of America copyright law. Any unauthorized usage of the text without express written permission of the publisher is a violation of the author's copyright and is illegal and punishable by law. All trademarks and registered trademarks appearing in this guide are the property of their respective owners.

For permission requests, write to the below address:
PYP Academy Press
141 Weston Street, #155
Hartford, CT 06141

The opinions expressed by the Author are not necessarily those held by PYP Academy Press.

Ordering Information: Quantity sales and special discounts are available on quantity purchases by corporations, associations, and others. For details, contact the author at www.ettyburk.com

Edited by: Karen Ang, Chloë Siennah
Character and concepts created and designed: Esther P. Burk
Illustrated by: Sushmita Singh and Amal Raj
Cover design by: Nelly Murariu
Typeset by: Nelly Murariu

Printed in the United States of America.
ISBN: 978-1-955985-82-6 (paperback)
ISBN 978-1-955985-84-0 (hardcover)
ISBN: 978-1-955985-83-3 (ebook)

Library of Congress Control Number: 2022916888

First edition, January 2023.

The information contained within this book is strictly for informational purposes. The material may include information, products, or services by third parties. As such, the Author and Publisher do not assume responsibility or liability for any third-party material or opinions. The publisher is not responsible for websites (or their content) that are not owned by the publisher. Readers are advised to do their own due diligence when it comes to making decisions.

The advice and strategies found within may not be suitable for every situation. This work is sold with the understanding that neither the author nor the publisher are held responsible for the results accrued from the advice in this book.

Publish Your Purpose is a hybrid publisher of non-fiction books. Our authors are thought leaders, experts in their fields, and visionaries paving the way to social change—from food security to anti-racism. We give underrepresented voices power and a stage to share their stories, speak their truth, and impact their communities. Do you have a book idea you would like us to consider publishing? Please visit PublishYourPurpose.com for more information.

A portion of the profits from this book will be dedicated to helping programs and initiatives that prevent bullying and discrimination.

To learn more about the author and for additional resources to facilitate this critical discussion, please visit **ettyburk.com**.

How to Use the Book

To help facilitate the discussion on differences, we included feeling and thinking questions and a glossary to help younger readers.

Parents, caregivers, therapists, and educators can use this story and these questions for children of all ages in order to discuss the critical and sensitive areas of inclusion, belonging, and acceptance. Organizations can also use this story as a tool in their DEIB training.

An educational and training supplement is also available. It includes plans and activities to integrate this meaningful story into a social, emotional, inclusion, and anti-bullying curriculum.

Please feel free to connect with Etty at **ettyburk.com** on how to include Aaron into your DEIB and anti bullying curriculum, or with any questions or for more information on the educational and training supplements.

Etty looks forward to talking with parents, therapists, educators, as well as organizational leaders and trainers. She is available to facilitate sessions and discussions on belonging and acceptance. Etty can also customize plans to incorporate Aaron's story into your school or educational system's social cognition curriculum.

This book is dedicated to the Aaron in each of us.

Let's help them shine!

Table of Contents

Prologue	XIII
Chapter 1	XVI
Chapter 2	8
Chapter 3	14
Chapter 4	18
Chapter 5	26
Chapter 6	30
Chapter 7	34
Chapter 8	38
Chapter 9	42
Chapter 10	48
Chapter 11	52
Chapter 12	60
Epilogue	63
Feeling and Thinking Questions	67
A Note from the Author	69
Selected Glossary	71
Acknowledgments and Gratitude	75
About the Author	78
Additional Resources and Connecting with Etty	79

*Glossary words are set in **bold** the first time they appear in the book. Specific Glossary Premium words are set in **purple bold** the first time they appear in the book.

Prologue

Once upon a time (and not too long ago), something incredible happened to forever change our small country of **Premium**…

"Hooray for Aaron the great! Our hero!" the crowds shouted.

Rays of the bright, warm sun playfully skipped across the Premium crowds. Like tall stems of shiny amethysts, the perfect purple Premiums clapped and cheered.

"Aaron, you're the best!" his friends called out.

Aaron, round, small, and emerald green, proudly rode by in the special golden chariot. "What an awesome day for a grand parade!" Aaron exclaimed as he waved back at all the purple Premiums.

Passing by his parents, he heard them tell everyone around them, "Aaron is our son, and we are so proud!"

The smell of freshly baked chocolate chip cookies and cotton candy filled the air. Aaron watched as colorful green and purple balloons lazily drifted across the clear, blue sky toward the—

Chapter 1

***D**ON, DON, TELARUN! DON, DON, TELARUN! DON, DON! DON, DON!*

Aaron lifted his heavy, sleepy head halfway up from his pillow as his get-me-up alarm clock rang.

DON, DON, TELARUN! DON, DON, TELARUN! DON, DON! DON, DON!

Rubbing his blue eyes, Aaron mumbled, "Alarm, turn off."

"I hate when I can't finish a good dream," he said while yawning.

Aaron slowly got out of his purple bed and turned off his make-me-feel-safe night light.

"Not that I'm scared of the dark. It's just nice to see stuff at night so I know there's nothing unexpected there," he said to himself.

As he washed up and got dressed, he hoped that his mom would tell him that they canceled school today.

AARON THE DIFFERENT

"Aaron, please hurry up or you will miss breakfast. You don't want to be late for school," his mom called out.

Aaron dragged his feet down the stairs and into the bright yellow and white kitchen.

"Mom, maybe school will be better today. Maybe someone will like me," Aaron whispered. Aaron always hoped for better days in school, but they never seemed to come.

"You are perfect the way you are!" she told him as she gave him a big hug.

Aaron smiled bravely as he headed to the door to catch the orange school airbus. On his way out, he made sure to grab an extra apple for his classmate Jessie. Sometimes Jessie didn't bring lunch to school. Aaron hated to see his friend hungry and unhappy, so he always tried to bring him something to eat.

CHAPTER 1

Eight-year-old Aaron lives in the country of Premium on the planet of **Astron**.

Astron is part of the many planets and stars of the **Harmonium Galaxy**. Our planet is famous for the seven deep red moons that orbit it every month. Some say that Astron looks similar to planet Earth from the Milky Way Galaxy. Like Earth, Astron has large areas of land surrounded by bright blue pools of running water. Fields of **different** shades of green and many huge brown and gray mountains cover the planet. Premium is located in the southern hemisphere of our beautiful planet and is filled with warm, sunny days and cool, crisp nights.

AARON THE DIFFERENT

To Aaron, everyone around him was tall and purple, while he was small and green. Even his family members did not look like him. Aaron's mom, dad, brother Bill, and sister Laura were all shades of violet and seemed as tall as young trees. They represented what was thought to be the best of Premium.

CHAPTER 1

"There he goes," his tall purple neighbors often said, shaking their lavender heads as Aaron passed them on the street.

"But Mom, why does he look like a little green ball?" asked some of the neighborhood children.

"Don't talk so loudly. He might hear you. Try not to stare," some of the Premium adults whispered to their children.

Aaron became very sad and embarrassed when he heard what others said about him. But he tried to hold his head as high as he could and kept on going.

In school, Aaron's teacher was Mrs. Padlock. She was tall and purple with curly red hair. She was very proud to be a purple Premium.

"Oh, there's the round green one," she said as Aaron walked in the room.

Aaron rolled his eyes and went to his seat.

"I remember when classrooms were *properly* purple," she continued as she took attendance.

"This day does not look like it will be any better," Aaron muttered to himself.

CHAPTER 1

Chapter 2

At dinner, Aaron's older brother Bill asked him, "Hey little brother, how was school today?"

Looking up, Aaron answered, "They tried to paint me Premium purple in art class again. Mrs. Padlock laughed and said that they just wanted to make everything Premium perfect."

Aaron's sister Laura cried out, "What? That's not fair! You're like the amazing color of the leaves on the trees. You don't need to be purple to be special. Some Premiums can be so stupid!"

Aaron couldn't meet their eyes. "I even had to miss recess because I wanted to wash off the paint. Coach Emmett was the only one who tried to help me. He brought me my towel and gym clothes so that I could change into something clean."

AARON THE DIFFERENT

"It sounds like you had a very difficult day. What happened to you today was wrong. We will call the principal again," Aaron's mom told him.

Aaron climbed off the chair and ran out of the dining room crying, "It doesn't even matter what you guys think or do! Everybody at school is so mean. Why do they want me to be like *them*? Why can't they just like me for who *I* am? I feel so alone!"

Aaron's family looked at each other and shook their heads sadly.

"Excuse me," Bill said as he left the table and ran up the stairs.

"Hey, Aaron. Let's talk it out. Don't let them get to you!" Bill called out after him.

"Leave me alone! You don't understand what it's like to be me!" sobbed Aaron as he slammed the bedroom door.

CHAPTER 2

AARON THE DIFFERENT

Later that night, Aaron's parents rested on the sofa while admiring their children's shelves of artwork, pictures, and trophies.

CHAPTER 2

"I love Aaron exactly the way he is, but he is not like his brother and sister. He is not like other perfect purple Premiums. Being different makes it so much harder for him. I see how sad he gets and how hard he tries to fit in," Aaron's mom said quietly. She quickly turned away from Aaron's shelf that was partly filled with his drawings and family pictures.

"He will use his talents. I believe in Aaron. You will see. Aaron will find his way to shine," replied his dad.

"Yes, he will," his mom agreed.

Chapter 3

The next day, in the Premium Purple schoolhouse, Mrs. Padlock greeted the children. "Good morning, my perfect purple Premiums. As part of our yearly Premium history celebrations, we will now discuss the important history of the perfect purple Premium."

AARON THE DIFFERENT

"Our special ancestors landed in Astron seven thousand and seventeen years ago. It was decided by these wise and knowing Premiums that the best Premiums are tall and purple. I have always been proud to be a perfect purple Premium and all of you should also be proud!"

Aaron slowly raised his hand and called out, "Who really decided this? Was *everyone* purple back then? Why is it so important to be purple? Can't you be an important Premium and make a difference while being small, round, and green—like me?"

A hush came over the classroom. The other children began to whisper to each other.

"There he goes again."

"Can't he just **accept** what's right? Why does he have to ask those things?"

"My mom says that I shouldn't play with him because he is green."

"My parents say the same thing."

Jessie looked down at his desk while holding the apple that Aaron had given him earlier. *Why can't they let Aaron be Aaron? He is always nice to me*, Jessie thought while trying not to make eye contact with anyone, especially Aaron. *I wish I had the courage to stand up for him.*

CHAPTER 3

Aaron slowly lowered his hand. He blinked away the tears that he hoped no one saw. He felt so let down by his teacher and classmates.

Mrs. Padlock wouldn't answer his questions and instead sent Aaron to the principal for disrupting the class. Aaron tried to stand as tall as he could and walked out of the classroom. The principal immediately sent Aaron home from school for the day with a note for his parents.

Chapter 4

Walking home from school, Aaron mumbled, "It is so hard being me. I can't seem to do anything right. I look different from the other Premiums. I don't think the same way. I just don't seem to fit in. Even Jessie doesn't seem to care. Why can't they just like me for me?"

Aaron knew he should have gone straight home, but he didn't want to. Since he had extra time and wanted to cheer himself up, he decided to visit his forest friends.

Usually Aaron saw his friends after school, while his mom and dad proudly watched Bill and Laura play on their sports teams. Aaron had tried out for the different teams at school, but he was never big enough or purple enough to be accepted by any team. Not being included was not easy for Aaron, but he found other places to go.

Aaron would sneak over to the edge of the forest to spend time with his strange and colorful friends, the **sunmoonies** and **myrtledockers**. The three-eyed sunmoonies were covered with rainbow-colored spikes that reflected the sunlight. The six-legged myrtledockers had two long, black split tongues. They were a bit scruffy, and they looked like their long bodies were loosely wrapped in shimmering blue and red diamond-shaped scales.

On that day, Aaron happily called out to his forest friends while running across the empty field through the thick, long blades of yellow and green grass.

"Hello, everyone. I am here!"

The creatures quickly jumped and slithered on Aaron and greeted him with nuzzles, grunts, and licks.

"Aw. Come on, guys. Stop," chuckled Aaron, tumbling onto the soft grass. "That tickles! So, what do you want to do today? What are we going to explore?"

"Let's explore some more tunnels," the sunmoonies squealed as their three eyes blinked.

"Yeah! Don't forget the caves!" roared the myrtledockers while stomping their six feet.

Even though Aaron was not really that comfortable in the dark, he still bravely explored the dim caves and tunnels with his friends. Aaron trusted them and knew that they would have his back.

The sunmoonies and myrtledockers were kind to Aaron and said things like, "The light you need is *within* you. In time, you will shine so bright that others shall finally see."

My friends seem very wise, but sometimes what they say is a bit mysterious and weird, Aaron thought to himself.

Aaron and his friends explored many narrow, deep, and winding tunnels that were connected to the large underground caves. During their adventures, the sunmoonies and myrtledockers introduced Aaron to the important secrets of the caves and taught him all about the tunnels. They explained where to go and how to not get lost. Aaron also liked to share what he knew about caves with his friends.

"Hey! Look at those amazing shapes hanging from the top of the cave," squealed the sunmoonies.

"Yeah! Aren't they great? Those are called **stalactites**. They take a long time to get that

large. They are made from evaporated water and **minerals**," Aaron explained.

"What about these incredible icicles that look like they're growing from the cave floor?" roared the myrtledockers.

"I know, right? Those are called **stalagmites** and they develop over time by water with minerals that drip to the bottom of the cave," Aaron replied.

"They look like upside-down stalactites!" squealed the sunmoonies.

Using his favorite glow-in-the-dark pen (which he also used to light the way), Aaron carefully drew maps of all the different tunnels in his journal. He also wrote down the exciting facts he learned about each of the tunnels.

AARON THE DIFFERENT

While exploring, the sunmoonies and myrtledockers reminded Aaron, "When you get to a tunnel that connects two caves, the right way to go is *left*."

"Wow! Here you guys go again with your mysterious advice!" Aaron said while laughing.

After a few hours of exploring, Aaron realized he had to head home. He did not want his family to worry about him and he wanted to make sure that there was plenty of time to get home before dark.

"I have to go home now. But I can't wait to spend more time with all of you. I am so lucky to have you as friends," he said with a smile.

"We are the lucky ones," squealed the sunmoonies as the myrtledockers roared in agreement.

On his way home, Aaron saw a neighbor struggling to carry some heavy packages. "I can help you with those packages, Mr. Adams," Aaron offered. He then worked really hard to carry the boxes.

"Wow! Thanks, Aaron. I did not think you were strong enough!" exclaimed Mr. Adams.

"Neither did I," Aaron replied, smiling.

Afterward, Aaron continued to kick the pebbles all the way home while playing with the note from

CHAPTER 4

his principal. He guessed that his parents were going to be very mad.

He was right.

They were upset with Aaron for getting in trouble at school. They were also very upset with Aaron for not telling them that he left to spend time with his forest friends. But they were very, very upset with the principal and Mrs. Padlock for what had happened and for how badly Aaron was treated at school.

"Aaron, we will be talking to the principal and Mrs. Padlock later today. How they treated you was so disappointing and totally unacceptable! But please try not to get into trouble at school. Also, you *must* let us know where you are and when you are spending time with your forest friends," his mom told him as his dad nodded in agreement.

Aaron was glad that his parents understood how he was feeling, but he still felt sad about being different.

Chapter 5

In school the next day, Mrs. Padlock announced, "I hope everyone remembered that today, the entire class is going on a special adventure. We will be visiting the famous Premium Cavernous Cave."

"Yay!" yelled the children, as they jumped up and down in their seats.

"Now, now children," Mrs. Padlock said, "We must maintain order. The airbuses are picking us up in a few minutes."

As the happy children started running down the stairs screaming, Mrs. Padlock reminded them, "Please march down the stairs slowly, in an orderly line with your assigned buddy." But they did not seem to hear her.

AARON THE DIFFERENT

Aaron was assigned to walk down the stairs with Mrs. Padlock instead of a classmate, but he was too excited about the trip to care. The airbuses transported them to the Premium Cavernous Cave at the edge of the forest. Aaron immediately recognized the fields and smiled to himself.

The children and teachers got off the orange airbuses in an orderly line. Outside the rocky cave opening, white signs with black and red letters stated: **CAVES CAN BE DANGEROUS, AND ALL VISITORS NEED TO STAY ON THE MARKED PATHS.**

"Hello, everyone! My name is Mr. Limestone and I am your cave guide for today. Yes, that is my name! Limestone—like the type of rock that is made up of bits of animal shells," the guide said.

"Cool name," said Jessie. Some of the children began to laugh.

Mr. Limestone added, "We will now go into the Premium Cavernous Cave. Everyone must stick together and follow the rules. Caves can sometimes be dangerous. And you should know that your phones and communication devices will not work in the cave. So put them away so you can watch where you're going!"

While Mr. Limestone talked, the children looked at the cave.

"Look how huge and tall it is!"

"Awesome!"

"This is going to be amazing!" cried the Premium children.

Chapter 6

Tall, steep, gray slopes surrounded the cave's entrance. Giant rocks in all shapes and sizes covered the outside walls. Tiny blue, yellow, and orange plants grew from inside the many cracks of the stones and sparkled like shiny jewels.

Guided by Mr. Limestone, the Premium children and their teachers walked down the paved path and entered the dimly lit cave entrance.

"Your eyes will get used to the dark. But do not worry. We also have a few large lanterns," Mr. Limestone said reassuringly.

I am glad I have my special glow-in-the-dark pen, thought Aaron.

Shades of brown, gray, and green covered the inside walls of the dark and chilly cave.

"Most caves develop naturally over a long time by running water wearing down the rocks. We see different shapes of rocks in different colors. All of them are important for the cave," explained Mr. Limestone.

With mouths and eyes opened wide, the children looked up and down at the patterns of rocks and large formations as they continued on the path, going deeper into the winding cave.

AARON THE DIFFERENT

"Hey, look! Those are stalactites and stalagmites!" cried Aaron.

"That is correct! The cone-shaped rocks that look like icicles growing down from the tall ceilings of the cave are called stalactites," explained Mr. Limestone.

"I hope they don't fall on us," one of the children said nervously.

Mr. Limestone smiled at the children and continued his explanation. "The cone-shaped rocks that grow upward from the floor of the cave are called stalagmites."

"I hope I don't fall on them! They look sharp," another one of the children said anxiously while backing away.

CHAPTER 6

Finally, the children stopped walking and stared at the different, strange, and fantastic shapes in the cave. Then they began picking up different rocks from the cave's floor and examining them.

"Wow! My rock is shiny and has little bumps all over it."

"My rock has sparkles."

"Mine glows in the dark."

"Mine is smooth and has tiny dots."

"They are so different."

"That's right! What makes a rock different can make it even more interesting and special. They are *all* an important part of the natural process of our cave. These beautiful rocks and shapes take a long time to develop. They can be made up of solid crystal minerals and even mud. Sometimes rocks are also made of **fungus**, which is a type of living thing, but not a plant or an animal," Mr. Limestone smiled while pointing to the different types of rocks.

"Wow," whispered some of the Premium children.

"Yuck," whispered some of the others.

All of a sudden, deep rumblings and crackling sounds were heard throughout the cave. The floors and walls began to gently shake.

Chapter 7

"All is fine, everyone," Mr. Limestone told the children, "This happens from time to time in our caves. Let us continue on our tour."

But the trembling of the cave's floors and walls became stronger! The rumblings got louder! The children and teachers began to sway, stumble, and fall!

Suddenly, a booming **avalanche** of large rocks tumbled down across the entrance of the cave. Then the rocks stopped falling.

Everything went silent and dark.

"Oh no!"

"Help me up!"

AARON THE DIFFERENT

"I'm on the dirty ground!"

"I want to get out!"

"Please stay calm!" Mrs. Padlock yelled over the children's cries as she tried to keep order. "Teachers, please have all the children sit down on the side of the path while Mr. Limestone checks the condition of the cave."

The children began whispering to each other.

"What is going to happen to us?"

"Maybe this is just part of the tour?"

"Do you think we will ever get out of this cave?!"

"I'm not scared at all."

"I'm afraid."

A few minutes later, Mr. Limestone approached Mrs. Padlock and said, "The falling rocks blocked the entrance to the cave! As you know, our phones and communication devices do not work here. We are in an awful situation and can't get help!"

Mrs. Padlock sat down, put her head in her hands, and **wept**, "This is very bad! I don't know how we are going to get out!"

CHAPTER 7

Chapter 8

At the same time, Aaron recognized the cave. *This is one of the caves I explored with my friends,* thought Aaron as he took his journal out from his shirt pocket. Using his glow-in-the-dark pen, he looked over his many drawings and maps. The teachers were very busy talking to Mr. Limestone, so they did not see Aaron crawling away.

I need to find the tunnel that can lead us out of the cave, thought Aaron.

Aaron crawled on his knees, going further and further down the cave's spooky, winding path. He nervously climbed over piles of dirt and pushed away sharp rocks that were blocking his way. He kept his glow-in-the-dark pen turned on to help him see. Based on his notes, Aaron knew the tunnel should be close by.

AARON THE DIFFERENT

Sliding his hands up and down the rocky and bumpy walls, Aaron suddenly felt the tunnel entrance!

"This is it! I found the tunnel that I used before, and I know it will lead us outside!" Aaron cried out.

"Mrs. Padlock! Mrs. Padlock!" Aaron called as he ran back to where the teachers were talking. "I know how we can get out of here! I found the tunnel that will lead us to the fields near the entrance of the cave."

Mrs. Padlock and the teachers just stared at Aaron in silence.

Mr. Limestone looked at them all and said, "Hey, everyone. Let's see what Aaron's figured out. Why don't you show us the tunnel you found? Please use one of our lanterns and lead us there."

Happy and proud to be able to help, Aaron led them to the tunnel entrance that he found.

CHAPTER 8

The children, teachers, Mrs. Padlock, and Mr. Limestone all stood around the small, round tunnel entrance. The adults bent down to try to get into the tunnel, but they could not. Their tall purple bodies simply did not fit in the small tunnel.

"Who can fit in there?" whispered the children. Even though they also tried, all the children were too tall and couldn't fit through the tunnel either.

"I can do this," Aaron declared. "I can fit and I know the way out."

They all turned around and looked at Aaron with surprise—and hope.

Mrs. Padlock gently placed her hands on Aaron's shoulders. "Aaron, you are the only one who can do this. Please go and get help. But be careful!"

The children moved out of the way so Aaron could pass. Jessie patted him on the back and said, "Good luck, Aaron. You can do this. I believe in you."

Aaron tried to smile bravely and said, "Thanks, Jessie. Don't worry, everyone. I will get help!"

Chapter 9

Aaron took a deep breath and entered the dark tunnel. There wasn't enough space to use Mr. Limestone's large lantern. Luckily, Aaron had his glow-in-the-dark pen with him.

"This is the first time I am doing this by myself, but I can do this," Aaron whispered.

He would have felt a lot better if the tunnel was not so gloomy and dim. Through the creepy shadows, Aaron began to follow the winding twists and turns, going deeper and deeper into the tunnel and further away from the cave.

After a while, the gloomy shadows began to flicker across the tunnel.

"What's happening?" Aaron cried.

All of a sudden, it was pitch black. The glow-in-the-dark pen had stopped working!

"Oh no! What should I do? Should I try to go back to the cave? Or should I continue on in the dark?"

Then he thought about his forest friends and their adventures together in the caves and tunnels. He remembered them saying, "The light you need is *within* you. In time, you will shine so bright that others shall finally see."

He thought about the scared children who were stuck in the cave.

"I will not give up! I have done this before, so I can do it again. I will figure out how to get them out of the cave. I am scared, but I know I can handle this!"

CHAPTER 9

So he continued.

Sometimes Aaron could stand up in the tunnel. Sometimes he needed to crawl. Sometimes he needed to clear the path of stones and dirt to move forward. But no matter what, he kept on going!

Suddenly, the tunnel split into two paths. Aaron had to figure out which way to go.

Aaron was very tired and wanted to rest, but he knew he had to stay awake. He sat down and tried to remember his maps and notes. Aaron closed his eyes. He took a few deep, long breaths to try to calm down and think more clearly.

After a few minutes, Aaron remembered what the sunmoonies and myrtledockers always told him: When you get to a tunnel that connects two caves, the right way to go is *left*.

So he got up, went to the left, and kept on moving. That part of the tunnel was very narrow. At times, Aaron had to crawl on his knees or get on his stomach and slither like a snake just to get through. Climbing over the sharp rocks, he scraped his knees and cried out in pain.

"This is taking me a long time. But I need to keep on going!" Aaron kept telling himself as he wiped his dripping forehead with his torn sleeve.

"Oh no!" Aaron yelled as he tripped over a rock and began tumbling head-over-heels down a very steep slope.

"Ahhhhhh!"

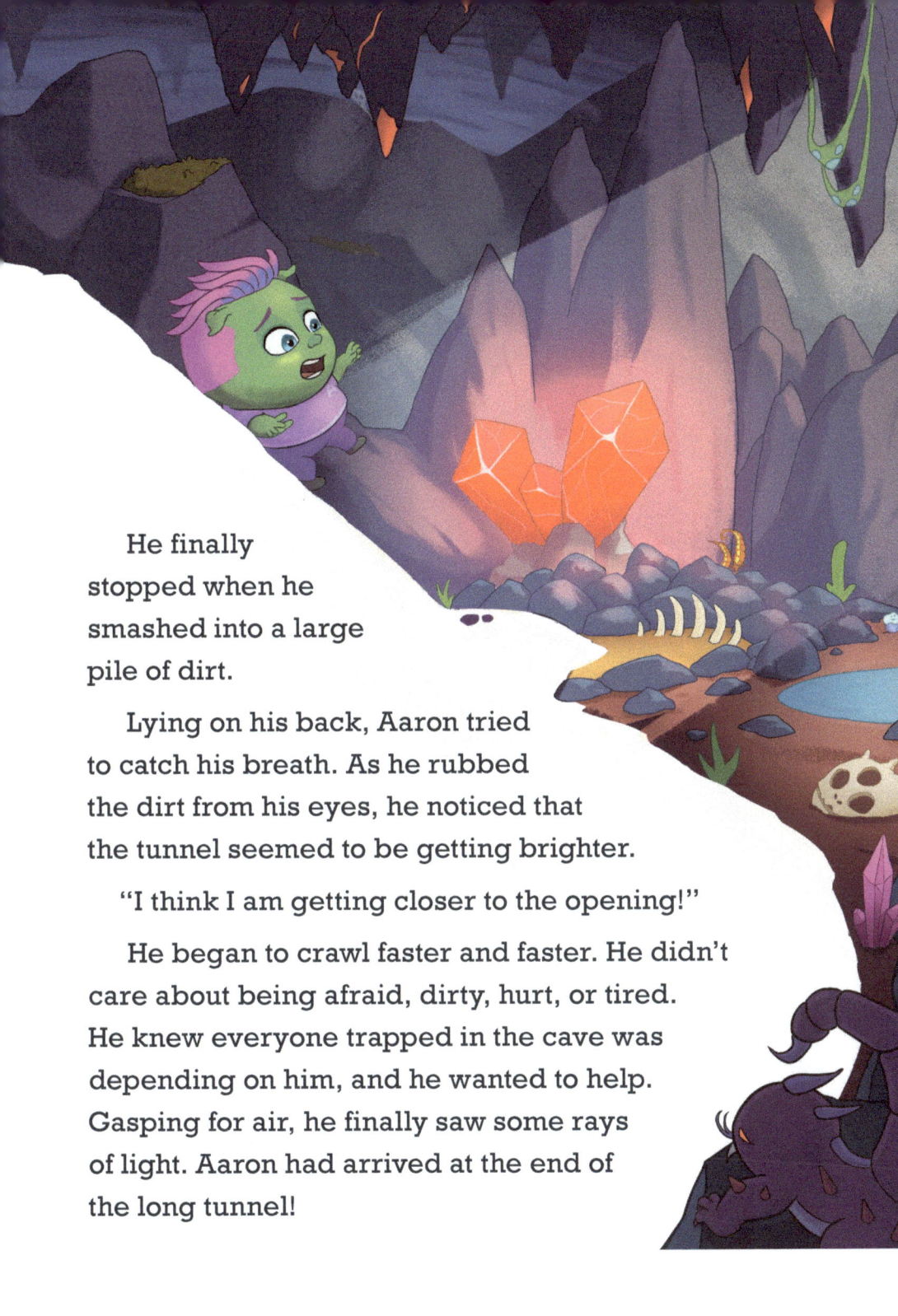

He finally stopped when he smashed into a large pile of dirt.

Lying on his back, Aaron tried to catch his breath. As he rubbed the dirt from his eyes, he noticed that the tunnel seemed to be getting brighter.

"I think I am getting closer to the opening!"

He began to crawl faster and faster. He didn't care about being afraid, dirty, hurt, or tired. He knew everyone trapped in the cave was depending on him, and he wanted to help. Gasping for air, he finally saw some rays of light. Aaron had arrived at the end of the long tunnel!

Chapter 10

Aaron ran out of the tunnel, covered with dirt and sweat. His arms and legs were scratched and bleeding. His shirt and pants were torn, but he didn't care.

Up the road to the parking lot he ran, surprising the airbus drivers.

"Call the police! Call the fire department! It's an emergency! My classmates, teachers, and Mr. Limestone are stuck in the cave! There was a loud noise, and then the rocks fell down around us! The entrance is blocked! We need help! Now!" Aaron yelled.

The Premium police and fire department came quickly to help. It took a very short time for the avalanche to be reported on the news. Different Premiums arrived to assist from all over the small country. Some even brought special trucks to move the giant rocks.

Worried families and friends of those trapped inside the cave also came to help. Aaron's family ran over to him and squeezed him tightly. Relieved, they spoke over one another.

AARON THE DIFFERENT

"We were so scared."

"We are so glad that you are okay."

"We are so very proud of you, Aaron."

Aaron's dad reached out and gently held his hand. He felt so thankful to see Aaron that he could not even get the words out.

Working together with Aaron, everyone helped move the smaller rocks one by one for many hours. The huge trucks moved the larger rocks.

When the darkened sky was sprinkled with shiny stars, they finally created an opening large enough for the children, teachers, and Mr. Limestone to escape. The children, tired, scared, and covered in dirt, ran out crying. The adults walked out slowly, looking shocked.

Mr. Limestone cried out when he saw Aaron. "Aaron, you did it! You figured it out, and you got us the help we needed!"

"Aaron, you were the only one who could fit in the tunnel and get us help. Thank you!" exclaimed Mrs. Padlock.

CHAPTER 10

Jumping and cheering, the children ran over to Aaron.

"Yay! Aaron saved us!"

Jessie gave him a high-five and said shyly, "You are a great friend!"

Eyes lowered, Aaron blushed a light shade of lime. "Wow, I think they really like me," Aaron said softly.

Chapter 11

News stations from all across Astron talked about Aaron. "Aaron, the brave, small, round, emerald green boy who was true to himself, not only figured out how to save the children and teachers of the Premium school, but had the courage to make it happen," the news reporters announced.

A week later, at the special ceremony, the president of Premium, Mr. Herman Goodwill, presented Aaron with a giant **tourmaline** trophy. It sparkled green and purple and was engraved with words that read:

For Aaron,
You taught us to value and appreciate what makes us different, and that Premium Perfection comes in all colors, shapes, and sizes.

President Goodwill then declared, "I am also proud of all the perfect Premiums who worked together to save the children and teachers. In honor of Aaron's bravery and quick thinking, and for all those who helped him, we will hold a grand parade! Also, next Monday, all schools will celebrate with a day off!"

The children cheered, "Aaron, you are the best," and lifted him high on their shoulders. Aaron raised his head as tall as he could and smiled proudly.

CHAPTER 11

The day of the parade finally arrived, and it was warm and bright. There were orange, red, and blue butterflies gently gliding over pink, yellow, and purple flowers. The black and green birds with yellow wings gently flew above the butterflies. Then, like bright gems of many colors, shapes, and sizes, the beautiful Premium crowds began to line the roads. They carried green "I Love Aaron" banners and waved "Aaron is the Perfect Premium" flags.

"Come on now! Let us move quickly if we are to get good spots for the parade," the Premium parents and caregivers said as the chorus of children shouted excitedly.

"I can't wait to see Aaron!"

"Did he really save the children?"

AARON THE DIFFERENT

"Wow, I want to be just like Aaron."

The sides of the roads quickly filled up with the happy Premium crowds and the parade began! The school bands from all around Premium proudly marched and danced down the street wearing their shiny and colorful green and purple uniforms. The marching bands took turns playing their drums, horns, tubas, **xylophones**, triangles, and cymbals.

"Hooray for Aaron the perfect Premium, our amazing hero!" the school bands sang and danced.

The rays of the glowing sun playfully skipped across the colorful Premium crowds. Surrounded by his friends, the sunmoonies and myrtledockers, Aaron—round, small, and emerald green—proudly rode the golden chariot with his feet dangling from the seat.

CHAPTER 11

"Aaron, you are the best," the Premium crowds shouted as Aaron waved to them.

"Aaron, we love you!" the crowds cheered and clapped.

"Can I take a picture with you?"

"No! Me first."

"No, me," cried the children standing at the side of the road.

Aaron's mom and dad held each other tight and waved at Aaron. They did not stop smiling. "We are so proud of our Aaron for finding the way!" they said to all the Premiums that were standing around them.

The smell of freshly baked chocolate chip cookies and cotton candy filled the air. Colorful green, purple, red, blue, and yellow balloons lazily drifted across the clear blue sky.

"Way to go, Aaron!" cheered Bill.

"We are so proud of you. You are amazing!" Laura applauded.

Aaron looked at the crowds in a daze. Biting into a soft chocolate chip cookie, Aaron thought, *I still can't believe this is happening. This is even better than my dream!*

AARON THE DIFFERENT

The sunmoonies and myrtledockers climbed over and around him, nuzzling playfully while growling and licking. Aaron called out to his mom and dad, "What an awesome day for a grand parade."

CHAPTER 11

Chapter 12

Later that night, Aaron's parents rested on the sofa while admiring their children's shelves of pictures, trophies, and prizes.

"I am so proud of Aaron. He showed us that he can take care of himself," Aaron's mom said while looking at Aaron's shelf filled with framed newspaper clippings of Aaron's heroics.

"We are so lucky that he is not always like the other perfect Premiums. He is our perfect Premium blessing," replied his smiling father.

"Yes, our Aaron bravely faced the dark and found his way to shine. I am so proud that he does not give up and tries so hard!" responded Aaron's mom.

Hiding in the corner of the staircase high above the living room, Aaron quietly listened to his parents and smiled.

AARON THE DIFFERENT

I guess being me is not so bad, thought Aaron.
*I know that things will not always be this good.
But I made it through the dark tunnel myself, and
I am ready to face anything! But to be totally honest,
what I really want is another day off from school!*

Still smiling, Aaron got up and went to his room
while holding on to his favorite glow-in-the-dark pen.

And because of Aaron, our small country of
Premium was changed happily ever after.

Epilogue

Two months later...

Entries from Aaron's Journal

AARON THE DIFFERENT

Monday

Today, in art class, we had so much fun. Mrs. Padlock talked about drawing the perfect purple Premium and the whole class started yelling, "There is more to being a Premium than being purple!" We all began throwing paint across the room. We ended up covered in all the colors. Even Mrs. Padlock was covered in different colors of paint! At first, she looked so angry, but then she started to laugh! Awesome!

Tuesday

I am still so mad!! At recess today, some of the kids would not let me join their game because they said they still don't play with Premiums that are round and green. So not fair! Bill and Laura told me to talk to Coach Emmett. He always makes me feel better after I talk to him. I will keep you posted!

EPILOGUE

Wednesday

Today, Mrs. Padlock gave a history lesson based on the latest Premium history research, and guess what? There were Premiums who looked just like me when our ancestors landed in Astron. They were very important to setting up the new land! Can you believe it? Round, green Premiums making a difference!

Thursday

I tried again to get on the sports team but did not make it. This is the second time this year! I am just so upset not to get on any of the teams again. But I feel a little better knowing that I could try again next month. It was so much fun to be on the sports field with everyone else. Mom, Dad, Laura, Bill, and my forest friends were there to cheer me on. I felt so proud! I even have a team t-shirt that Coach Emmett gave to everyone who tried out for the teams! Coach Emmett also told everyone who did not make the teams that we are invited to join practice on Tuesdays after school. He said that practice will help us get better! I guess I can't win every time, even though I want to. But I will keep on trying!

AARON THE DIFFERENT

Friday

This week, my forest friends and I started a cave tour business called Cave Rock Tours! We will have our tours after school on Fridays. Today, Mr. Limestone, Jessie, Bill, Laura, Mom, and Dad were our first tour group! Bill and Laura even took off from their sports practice to go on the tour. So happy it worked out. Most of them could not fit into the tunnels, so we found other things that they could do. We wanted to make sure that they all had fun and that everyone could take part in the tour. Some of my friends from school have already signed up for next week's tour! Can't wait!!

Feeling and Thinking Questions

We can learn different things from Aaron's story. Below are some questions to explore. There are no right or wrong feelings or answers. If you want, you can also share them with a friend, parent, caregiver, or your teacher. You can also choose to use these questions in a **Book Club**. Maybe they will have their own feelings and thoughts to share, too!

1. Do you know someone who may sometimes feel like Aaron? What do you think being different feels like to them?

....
....
....

2. Why do you think others did not accept Aaron?

....
....
....

AARON THE DIFFERENT

3. What do you wish happened differently in this story?

....
....
....
....

4. Did you find any of Aaron's journal entries from the Epilogue surprising? If so, why?

....
....
....
....

5. What can each of us do to help those around us feel accepted and included?

....
....
....
....

A Note from the Author

Many stories in the world's long and recent history demonstrate the terrible impact of **bias**, bullying, and **discrimination**.

As an Organizational Psychologist, I focus on helping to create a place at work where people feel respected and safe and understand that they are valued. But, unfortunately, I see firsthand how discrimination plays out every day.

I know great work is already happening in **diversity**, **equity**, **inclusion**, and **belonging**, and I wanted to help focus this work on children.

I remember a girl who felt different and had difficulty making friends in school. She watched as others played and laughed every day and felt she could not join them. Then one day during playtime, a boy came over and asked her to join his game. The girl was so happy and slowly started to not feel so sad and alone. Over time, she began asking other kids to join in during playtime because she wanted to help others, just like the boy who helped her.

I was that little girl who felt different, and this act of kindness by this boy changed my life. Because of this powerful memory, I asked myself, "What could I do to help empower children to accept and **respect** differences and do this better than adults do today?"

I wanted to create a story supporting the critical mindful discussion around **tolerance**, acceptance, inclusion, and belonging. I believe strongly that we have the power to change things for the better if we all work together.

Our differences make each of us **distinct** and unlike anybody else. People can't always see what makes us feel different, but we would all like our differences to be accepted and respected.

Sometimes what makes others different or unique can make us feel uncomfortable. But it is vital to still figure out ways to be kind and include everybody, especially those who are typically excluded from a game or conversation. Then, we can all help someone else feel like a part of the group, welcomed and embraced as someone who truly belongs.

All acts of kindness are super powerful.

We are all part of this fantastic, ever-turning world. We all have the power to add value and make a real positive change.

So, here's the call to action! Here's where we can make a difference!

What can we do to help those around us feel accepted and included?

What can others do for you to help you feel accepted and included?

Now, imagine the amazing world we can create if all of us answer these questions loudly and proudly!

Imagine a world where it is normal to reach out and help someone feel like they belong!

I am excited and cannot wait to see what we can do together to help our world be the best it can be!

Selected Glossary

Glossary words are set in **bold** the first time they appear in the book.

accept: To act as if someone belongs; to receive someone or something willingly.

amethyst: A pale, bluish-purple color; also a type of purple quartz or stone.

Astron: A fictional planet where Aaron and the Premiums live; part of the **Harmonium Galaxy** and famous for the seven red moons that orbit it every month.

avalanche: A large number of rocks or amount of snow falling downward.

belonging: Being comfortable and feeling included and accepted.

bias: To prefer something (or someone) to something (or someone) else without any real reason.

differences/being different: All that makes us special, diverse, unique, and unlike others. We would like our differences to be respected. Sometimes other people can see what makes us different, and sometimes people cannot see what makes us different.

discrimination: Treating a person unfairly because of who they are or because they possess certain characteristics.

AARON THE DIFFERENT

distinct: Different, unique, or not the same.

diversity: Differences. People may be different in many ways, including race, religion, age, disabilities, language, culture, how they identify, and appearance.

emerald: A green mineral and a very precious stone.

equity: Making sure that everyone—regardless of who they are—has access to the same opportunities to grow and develop.

fungus: A living thing that is neither a plant nor an animal. When there is more than one fungus, they are called fungi. Some fungi are mushrooms, molds, truffles, and yeasts.

inclusion: Being a part of things and being welcomed and embraced as someone who belongs. Inclusion can happen everywhere!

limestone: A type of rock made up of bits of animal shells.

mineral: Forms that are usually solid and have a crystal structure. They are formed by natural processes.

myrtledockers: Fictional forest creatures with six legs, two split black tongues, and a long body with blue and red scales.

SELECTED GLOSSARY

Premium: The fictional country on the planet of Astron that Aaron lives in with his family, friends, and the rest of the Premiums. The word **premium** means something or someone that has higher quality.

respect: Showing kindness and being thoughtful of other things. Being respected means you feel valued or feel like you make a difference.

stalactites: Cone-like shapes that hang from the roof or side of a cave, formed by evaporated water that contains minerals.

stalagmites: Cone-like shapes rising from the cave floor like an upside-down stalactite. The shapes are formed by water containing minerals that dripped to the bottom of a cave.

sunmoonies: Fictional forest creatures with three eyes and rainbow-colored spikes.

tolerance: Being willing to accept or respect what is different in others, especially how they look, their beliefs, and customs.

tourmaline: A unique mineral rock that can have many colors, including green, pink, and blue that sometimes looks purple.

wept: To cry; shed tears.

xylophone: A musical instrument played by hitting a row of wooden bars with a mallet.

Acknowledgments and Gratitude

The world is a better place because of those who live their lives each day, showing us that we are all wonderfully different and can make a positive difference!

I am forever grateful to my parents, Sara and Leo Platovsky. Their love, encouragement, and belief in a moody and awkward girl knew no bounds. They taught me that obstacles are there to make your journey more fun and less boring as you figure out how to get past them. I am constantly in awe of their ability to move on and forgive even after experiencing the most racist horrors of our recent world history. Dad, I miss you so much every day.

To my talented and tolerant offspring, Elana and Meir, who showed me how to accept and understand Aaron more deeply. Elana, your incredible suggestions and perceptions became part of Aaron and his story. Meir, your short story in creative writing became Aaron's impetus and your ongoing insights added enormous value. You both are precious and provide deep joy and meaning to my life every day.

To my patient, understanding, and encouraging life partner, Dr. Robbie Burk, whose love, insights, and honesty keep me balanced. Thank you for believing in me (more than I believe in myself) and for all your ongoing "life support," as well as targeted edits and insightful ideas for Aaron. I love you.

My deep appreciation and thanks to Marilyn Meltzer, who guided and encouraged my story from its conception. I always looked forward to our tea meetings and discussions. Your expertise and wisdom influenced Aaron and me in many ways.

To my sister from another mother, Dr. Sara Barris, I trusted Aaron with you as a first reader before trusting others. You cheered Aaron and me on when we needed it most and shared with me pithy insights and advice, raising the quality and depth of my story. You even shared your family as reviewers, and to you and to them, I am forever grateful.

To Dr. Michal Stein and his amazing wife, Dr. Penelope Stein, and brilliant family, Sophie and Ariella. Thank you for your patience, encouragement, and your beautiful ideas. I am awed by the vital work you do for global diversity every day. You guys inspire me and I am so lucky to have you all in my life.

To my brother David and his son Benny who were taken away too soon, and to his fantastic family, Edit, Rivka, and Shlomo, you taught me about true acceptance and bringing dignity and compassion to living with differences. I am deeply thankful to each of you.

To my special friends, Fay Lindenfeld, Atara Sternman, and Dr. Laurie Gordon for their ongoing thoughtful and timely encouragement, patiently reviewing the seemingly endless versions, and giving me unique ideas. Your friendship is my lifeline.

Thanks to my guides and sherpas through the publishing processes: the awesome Jenn T. Grace and her amazing PYP team, Bailly Morse, Karen Ang, Chloë Siennah, and Nelly Murariu. I definitely would not have made it to the summit without you! Your editorial guidance and expertise helped me get Aaron to another level. I loved working with all of you!

Special thanks to Sushmita Singh and her partner Amal Raj, who patiently partnered with me through my many ideas and versions to make Aaron and Premium come alive with your imaginative illustrations. Your creative talents sparked life to my vision.

Last but certainly not least, deep appreciation to all my family, friends, teachers, mentors, professors, and colleagues who have helped me along this journey. I am truly blessed.

About the Author

Etty Burk is passionate about inclusion and respect in both her personal and professional life. As an Organizational Psychologist, she works on projects that reinforce her passion for creating inclusive environments and cultures where all feel valued, safe, and respected. In addition, Etty has partnered with leaders across various industries to create healthy organizations with happy and engaged employees. Etty obtained a Ph.D. in Psychology and Education from Columbia University.

Etty's passion for inclusion resulted in this story of tolerance, belonging, hope, and being unique. Etty currently lives in New York and is lucky to be part of a family of wonderfully different and unique humans.

Please feel free to connect with her at
ettyburk.com
She would love to hear from you!

Author Photo Credit: Rick Guidotti is the founder and director of POSITIVE EXPOSURE (positiveexposure.org), a non-profit organization that promotes a more inclusive world through award winning photography, film, and educational programs.

Additional Resources and Connecting with Etty

Parents, caregivers, therapists, and educators can bring this story into their homes and classrooms to facilitate the critical discussion around inclusion, belonging, and acceptance. Organizations can also use this book as a tool in their DEIB training. To help guide the discussion on differences, we included feeling and thinking questions in the book.

Schools, Libraries, Organizations

Special bulk rates are available for those who would like to use this book to facilitate the critical DEIB discussion with your students or teams. Learn more at ettyburk.com.

Free Online Resources

Etty has also created a collection of resources, including educational and training supplements with plans and activities to integrate this meaningful story into a social, emotional, inclusion, and anti-bullying curriculum. You can learn more about these and other resources at ettyburk.com.

Consulting, Facilitation, Speaking

Etty looks forward to talking with parents, therapists, educators, organizational leaders, and trainers. In addition, she is available to facilitate sessions and discussions on belonging and acceptance, and she can customize plans to incorporate Aaron's story into your school or educational system's social cognition curriculum.

Please connect with Etty at ettyburk.com for more information on how to include Aaron in your DEIB and anti-bullying curriculum and for speaking, facilitation, and consulting needs.

www.ingramcontent.com/pod-product-compliance
Lightning Source LLC
Chambersburg PA
CBHW041441010425
24428CB00009B/132